Glory

RESCUED, REDEEMED, TRANSFORMED

A COLLECTION OF ADVENT READINGS

Printed in the United States of America

Cover by: Victoria Hawkins

First Printed in October 1, 2020

ISBN:

Printed by Amazon.com

www.thisroadhome.com

Grace to you and peace from God our Father
and the Lord Jesus Christ,
Who gave Himself for our sins so that He might
rescue us from this present evil age,
according to the will of our God and Father,
to Whom be the Glory Forevermore. Amen.

Galatians 1:3-5

—

And it will be said in that day,
"Behold, this is our God
for Whom we have waited
that He might save us.
This is the Lord for whom we have waited;
Let us rejoice and be glad in His salvation."

Isaiah 25:6-9

Table of Contents

INTRODUCTION 7

MEET THE AUTHORS 13

DAILY READINGS 19

OBSERVING ADVENT AT HOME 97

THE ADVENT WREATH 103

WEEKLY FAMILY READINGS 107

ABOUT THE AUTHOR 128

Introduction

*G*lory. It is probably not the word you think of when you think of 2020. The world has been through a lot in the past months, and many people are still hurting– still experiencing the grief of lost loved ones, still trying to dig out from the rubble caused from lost jobs, storms, fires.

And yet here we are again. Another Advent season– one that many people doubted we would ever see.

This year I am more thankful than ever for Advent– for God's goodness in reminding us that His plans are always greater and that He is working out these plans in ways that we can't even imagine, much less see. How mindful we are of God's Word spoken to the prophet Isaiah: "For My thoughts are not your thoughts, nor are your ways My ways..." Isaiah 55:8.

One thing I should mention– this is not a book about Christmas. It's a book about Jesus. The more I have made Advent a part of my life, the more I have come to realize all that Advent means. Advent is all of it– Jesus' birth, His life, His death, His resurrection, and His return. There are many references to the Christmas story here, but in this book you will also find references to so much more about the life of our Savior.

This year the devotional readings are meant to be an encouraging reminder that God's plan for each of His children and His church leads us to glory. He has designed us for it from the very beginning–and He will not fail. The passage of Scripture that the book's title is taken from is 2 Corinthians 4:16-18. I encourage you to make this passage one that you commit to memory over the next few weeks. It will bring you comfort and strength. That verse reads:

"Therefore, we do not lose heart, but though our outer man is decaying, yet our inner man is being renewed day by day. For momentary, light affliction is producing for us an eternal weight of glory far beyond all comparison, while we look not at the things which are seen, but at the things which are not seen; for the things which are seen are temporal, but the things which are not seen are eternal."

What does it mean to be rescued, redeemed, and transformed? These three words encompass the life of every believer from the point of salvation until the Lord calls us home. Every believer has experienced that moment when God has rescued us out of the mess that sin has made of our lives. It's the point where we find ourselves facedown at the cross, humbled, helpless, and yet realize we are deeply loved and wanted by God, our Creator, our holy Father.

But He doesn't rescue us from one mess to let us go back into that same mess. No, that cross is where He has redeemed our souls. The word redemption carries with it the idea of our being purchased by God, not with payment, but by His great power. By the perfect sacrifice of His sinless Son He has exerted His power over the sin that has enslaved us in its bondage, and He has placed us in a position of honor in His family. No longer slaves to sin, His redemptive work makes us His children.

Many of the devotionals you will read in the following weeks talk about how this rescue and redemption has led to the transformation of lives. This is called sanctification. As God's redeemed children, we are set apart to be transformed, to be conformed to the image of Christ. Romans 12:2 says that this transformation begins with a change in the way that we think. Paul writes, "And do not be conformed to this world, but be transformed by the renewing of your mind...." We begin to see things from God's perspective. We understand more every day the joy and blessing that comes through obedience, humility, loving others, and spending time learning to know and love God. This process of transformation continues until we one day meet our Lord in glory— when we will be made completely whole for all eternity.

We can rejoice in this great message. There is no better news, no greater comfort to our souls than the message that Christ has come, Christ gave His life, Christ has risen, and Christ will come again.

Each year, proceeds from the sale of the Advent book project are donated to various ministries. I do this with the hope that you will take a look at what these ministries are doing and get involved either in serving or giving.

This year I am spotlighting two ministries. The first is Grasp International's ministry in Nairobi, Kenya, called **The Widows' Voices.** This ministry has developed as part of the Echoes of Mercy Mission, and serves to assist the widows in their area of the world in being successful by repairing their homes, giving them meals, and shining the light of Christ in their lives. You can find out more, donate, or volunteer to serve by visiting graspinternationalinc.com.

The second ministry is called **Purchased: Not for Sale.** This ministry is part of The Hub Ministry, based in Shreveport, Louisiana. **Purchased: Not for Sale** is actively involved in giving rescue, relationship, recovery, and resources to women and children experiencing sexual exploitation and sex trafficking in Shreveport, Las Vegas, Fort Worth, and Lafayette, Louisiana. You can read more about them at thehubministry.org.

This year's book is a collaborative effort, and I extend my deepest gratitude for those who have contributed: David and Christy Grantham, Debi Hutchens, John Myer, Jamie and Traci Powell, and Justin Stewart. Take a look at the "Meet the Authors" page to learn more about them. Their names are listed with the entries they contributed. You will be blessed. All other entries were written by me, and don't include a "written by" line.

I'd also like to thank my friend Tonya Lamb for sharing her testimony of with me. You will find her story on December 7. And, as always, my friend Victoria Hawkins has done another stellar job on book design. I can't recommend her enough, so look her up at victoriahawkinsdesign.com. Just not during September, because she's going to be busy with my Advent book!

As you read through the Scriptures and devotions this year, remember that God is intent on rescuing those He calls His own. He brings us through unthinkable anguish and hurt. He redeems us. He heals us. He loves us. And He transforms us. As you read through the devotionals this year, I hope that you will be reminded of this great truth, and that the Gospel will reach you in all the places of your heart and life that feel battered and alone.

Meet the Authors

i have been blessed to be surrounded by a very special "cloud of witnesses" in my life, and no matter how, or at what point the Lord has allowed our paths to cross on this journey home, they have blessed me, encouraged me, and exhorted me in some way.

The story of rescue, redemption, and transformation looks different in every life, and that is why I have asked these friends to share from their perspectives. Many of us have been rescued from a "religious life" of thinking that our good works are enough; some of us have been rescued from a not so religious life at all. The one thing we all have in common is that at one point in our lives we looked up at the cross of Christ and proclaimed our need for Him. We were rescued and redeemed at the foot of Calvary, and we are all in the process of being transformed.

Yes, I am blessed to have such faithful men and women walking this road to Glory with me. Here's the team that has shared their hearts with you this year:

David and Christy Grantham

 David and Christy are veterans in the ministry. David currently serves as pastor of Pinecrest Baptist Church in Cordele, Georgia. Christy teaches at Westfield Schools in Perry, Georgia. David also serves as President of Grasp International, and he and Christy are resident overseers at Stillwater Pastor Retreat in Arabi, Georgia. They have three adult children– Evan (Taylor), Logan

(Cara) and Sara Fogarty (Andrew), and one grandchild, Stephan Grantham.

- David — "Looking Forward to Glory," December 11
- Christy — "Mary's Song," December 21

Debi Hutchens

Debi is the author of two books, **Bypass in the Road: Journey of the Heart** and **Got a Hole in the Bottom of My Shoe but It Is Well with My "Sole."** She considers her family to be her greatest accomplishment. She and her high-school sweetheart and husband, Larry, have been married for over 47 years. They have four married children and nine "grand-blessings." Her heart's passion is sharing and encouraging others about the Lord, especially in such a time as this when many are seeking hope on their journey.

- "Desperate Faith: The Woman with the Issue," December 4
- "The Lord Has Done Great Things for Us," December 19

John Myer

John is currently serving as pastor at Grandview Christian Assembly, a church he planted in the Columbus, Ohio, area. He is the author of three books, **Shopping vs. Seeking: A Focused Approach to Finding a Church; Presence: Praying the Scriptures to Encounter the Glory of God;** and **Solid: An Indestructible Foundation for New Christians.** He also authors a blog, **bareknuckle.org**. Natives of Louisiana, He and his wife Aleisha have been married for over 30 years and have one adult daughter. For information about John's availability for your ministry event, contact him via his blog or his church's website at grandviewchristianassembly.org

- "More Thrilling, More Filling," December 23

Jamie and Traci Powell

Jamie and Traci have been serving in ministry together for almost 32 years. Jamie has served at FBC Perry for over 10 years. They met at Southwestern Baptist Theological Seminary in Ft. Worth, Texas, and have been married 31 years. Their daughter Kati and her husband Andrew Cannon are in pastoral ministry in Arizona, and their son, Caleb owns a welding business in Utah. They have one grandson, Elijah Cannon.

- Traci: "Open Up the Heavens," December 8 and "Rescue in the Storm," December 15
- Jamie: "Finally Some Good News," December 18

Justin Stewart

Justin and his family live on a small farm in middle Georgia where they practice regenerative agriculture and permaculture principles. He and his wife Ashley have been married for 11 years. They have two beautiful daughters, Kate (5), and Ellie (2).

- "An Adopted Lamb," December 1

No longer will you have the sun for light by day
Nor for brightness will the moon give you light;
But you will have the Lord for
An everlasting light,
And your God for your glory.
Your sun will no longer set,
Nor will your moon wane;
For you will have the Lord for
An everlasting light.
And the days of your mourning will be over.
Then all your people will be righteous;
They will possess the land forever;
The branch of My planting,
The work of My hands,
That I may be glorified.

Isaiah 60:19-21

Daily Readings

A Time to Prepare

Luke 2:10-14; Rev. 22:12-21

How do you even begin to approach a season like Advent in a year like 2020? We know these next few weeks are meant to remind us of hope, peace, joy, and love– but after all our world has experienced over the past year, can we even fully wrap our minds around those themes without a hesitation that wasn't there a year ago?

My answer is a resounding, "Yes!" Here is my go-to definition of Advent: The season of the year Christians prepare our hearts for the celebration of Christ's birth. It is a time for us to celebrate His coming into our hearts and our lives today, and a time to prepare ourselves in anticipation of His imminent second coming.

This year, more than ever, we are ready! Everything we have gone through over the course of this year has reminded us that this world is not where we as believers belong. It has re-ignited a spark in our hearts of longing to be in our eternal home. Truly we can throw off the shadows of fear and anguish and rejoice that we have a glorious future awaiting us.

However, being ready and being prepared are not the same thing, and in the days ahead I hope that you will also deeply examine your heart and life to determine how prepared you are.

COVID-19, politics, and civil unrest over what is being called systemic racism has monopolized our attention this year. But there is a deadlier virus than the Corona Virus. There is an issue deeper and more urgent than political battles. There is a problem more destructive than racism. The true prob em is sin– and we are all infected.

I know... when the term "sin" enters the conversation, a lot of people stop listening. It's not a popular term. The world's culture, ruled by Satan, minimizes and mocks the word. He has whispered in the ears of people everywhere that sin is for religious people, it's judgmental, and certainly not a key issue.

The truth is, the only thing that makes the news of Christmas Good News is the fact that sin is a problem that man can't conquer. It's good news because we no longer have to try. Jesus came to conquer it for us. Here in this world, in this generation, children are told from an early age how "good" they are, wrongs are brushed off as "mistakes," and justified, or blamed on others; yet in the heart of man he knows that all is not okay. We walk around with an invisible sense of guilt and shame that we don't have a name for, and that we don't know what to do with. So we cover it over with pride and arrogance and hatred, and numb it with drugs and alcohol and superficial relationships and material things. But that infection of sin keeps eating away at our souls.

You see, inherently we know there is a standard that we are not meeting. Being told that everything is fine and good creates spiritual frustration and confusion. And we will do anything to numb the pain of that frustration. The rate of failed marriages, along with the soaring rates of substance abuse, sexual perversions, and suicides are all indicators that we know that something is not right– no matter what we're told. We think, it can't be something as "simple" as sin.

But the holiness of God still demands justice, and that justice leads to eternal death in torment for unredeemed man, because

21

none of us can live up to His perfect standard. Oh, but the love of God— it provides mercy and grace, it provides redemption, and justification, and restoration. He rescues us out of the path of God's judgement— the execution of His justice— that will one day destroy all the rulers and Kingdoms of this world and establish the perfect, beautiful, and glorious Kingdom of God for all eternity. He transforms us from glory to glory. He remakes us as a potter works a lump of clay, over and over, until we are conformed into the image of His Son.

All of that begins when we finally agree with Him that our lives are ruled by sin, and we see just how filthy that sin is. No matter how good we may think we are, our own goodness can never reach deep enough to make us right with God.

But Jesus can, and Jesus did through the perfect sacrifice of His perfect life. He asks only that we trust Him and the work that He has done on our behalf.

Jesus conquered sin at the cross, and then He conquered death when He walked out of the grave three days later. One day soon, He will put an eternal end to the sin, sorrow, and sickness of this world when He returns to establish everlasting righteousness with His people. This is the Good News that our souls are longing for. It's the Gospel that drives away the frustrations and confusions deep in the spirit of man, filling us instead with all the goodness of being His forgiven, redeemed child.

Are you prepared for His return? You may not know how to answer that question today. You may answer with, "I hope so." Or "I think so." Eternity is too long and too close to step into it without complete assurance. I John 5:13 tells us that we can **know** that we have eternal life. But it must be settled this side of eternity.

In Revelation 22, twice Jesus promises, "I am coming quickly." There is great hope, and endless joy in that promise. I hope that you are prepared as well as ready. I hope that when you think of Christ's return it is with anticipation, not dread.

I hope that whatever struggles are facing you today,

that you will find a few moments of peace to celebrate

the good news of great joy that is the message of

Advent.

November 30

His Glorious Plan

Isaiah 9:6-7

So how was your day today? Stressful? Brutally busy and overwhelming? Did you have to stop at some point and catch your breath? Or was even breathing a luxury for you today?

Today I observed people around me so knotted up with tension, worry, and anxiety that not a speck of joy or gladness could be found in their countenance. Instead there was anger, fear, irritation, and resignation. I watched as drivers who were in such a hurry and full of impatience caused near-accidents on the highways as they raced to get to where they were going and to get there first.

Today I listened as people listed off the multitude of worries and troubles they are facing, and heard the anxiety in their voices rise as they wondered how they would get through it all– dreading the week before them.

The most wonderful time of the year? Not hardly!

Today, I tried to see this real world that we real people live in through the filter of Advent. This season that has been set aside for all believers to stop the usualness of life and just remember Jesus– His birth, His life, His death, His resurrection, His return.

This journey, this road home we are traveling, though difficult at times, was never meant to be filled with burdens we carry alone. It is not a contest to see how much we can bear before we break. It is meant to be a steady race with a Savior-Companion who loves us beyond measure and wants to be always in fellowship with us— if we will allow Him to be.

This Advent— just for these few holiest of holy days, can we make the conscious choice to put aside those things that compete for space in our hearts for just a little while, and think of Him? Can we make remembering our Savior our top priority, knowing that as He stepped down from Glory into the life of a tiny baby, He made us His priority? Can we be still for a little while and just remember Him? Not that we forget our own struggles; just that we see them through the filters of Bethlehem, of Golgotha, of Calvary, of the empty tomb.

And if we will quiet and still our spirits and listen to His voice, we will understand the power of the victory that Christ won for us— for our day to day usualness of life, and for all eternity. We will recall how He rescued us from the destiny of the perishing, we will observe His redemptive and transforming power in every aspect of our lives, and we will have the peace of those who have the certain hope of Glory.

Let Him change you this Advent.

Let this be the year that you give all of yourself

over to Him to do the great work in your life

that He so desires. He has a glorious plan for you.

December 1

An Adopted Lamb

Psalm 80:1-7, 17-19; John 10:11-18

Written by: Justin Stewart

All throughout scripture people are referred to as sheep. Having been around animals and livestock all of my life, I can tell you, that's not a compliment. Sheep are dumb! The twenty-third Psalm says a Good Shepherd leads his sheep beside still waters. Why is this important? Well, sheep are not good swimmers, but they aren't smart enough to realize it. They will run right into deep, swift water that will soak their wool and make them drown— unless their shepherd leads them beside calm, shallow waters where they can wade in and drink.

The Psalmist had a keen understanding of this when drawing the comparison between sheep and Joseph's descendants. In Psalm 80, the people of Israel were in a bad place. They had lost their way, as orphans with no one to care for them. The psalmist is begging God to come and rescue His people, but they had no idea just how intimate of a rescue it would be.

When a lamb is orphaned a good shepherd has to find a way to care for that lamb. Modern shepherds may use artificial milk and bottle feed the new lamb, but ancient shepherds didn't have that luxury. The fix in that time was much more personal. The shepherd would take the orphaned lamb, and wrap it in the skin of a stillborn or deceased lamb to cover its own scent. The hope was that the mother who delivered the stillborn lamb would smell the scent of her own lamb and accept the orphaned lamb as her own. Do you see the parallel?

In John 10, Jesus calls Himself the Good Shepherd who lays down His life for His sheep. He also says He has other sheep who are not a part of the main (Jewish) flock, but that He would bring them in, and make them a part of the same flock. For the people of Israel, and for us today, God didn't use a stillborn lamb, but rather, He sent His perfect Lamb to be intentionally sacrificed. That sacrificial Lamb would wrap us in His blood to cover our sin and allow us to become adopted children of God.

One of the most beautiful things about this Lamb is that, just as He says in John 10, He laid down His life as a sacrifice, but then He picked it back up again to continue to be our Good Shepherd. He is always there to lead us beside still waters, and He is just waiting for the Father to say, bring My children home!

This Advent season, let's focus on the Lamb,

the Lamb who was sacrificed to enable us

to be called children of God,

but more than that let us

focus on the risen Lamb of God

who is still our Good Shepherd, and

who is still coming back for His sheep.

Are you an adopted lamb?

December 2

Old Cast Iron Pot

2 Timothy 2:20-26

Brenda Gantt is my new favorite person. I am one of almost 800,000 followers this 73 year-old retired Alabama school teacher has on Facebook. And let me tell you, I am faithful. The first time I watched her, I was hooked. I can't wait to see what she has in store for us this Christmas season!

If you are not familiar with Mrs. Gantt, let me give you the run-down. In the early days of the pandemic, she recognized that a lot of wives and mothers were suddenly having to cook meals regularly and were struggling. One day she was making a pan of buttermilk biscuits, and decided to video herself in a tutorial. That video has been viewed well over a million times, and prompted Brenda to start a Facebook page to post more cooking how-to's.[1]

One night as I was struggling to fall asleep, I picked up my phone and opened Facebook. There on my feed was Brenda showing me how to take a rusty, dirty old cast iron pot and restore it to usefulness. She scrubbed and scrubbed and rinsed that pot until it was clean. After multiple scrubbings, she let it dry. And then she put it on the stove and fried some bacon in it.

I was doubtful— fully expecting that bacon to stick into an impossible mess. But she explained that as the iron molecules heated, they expanded, allowing the grease from the bacon to penetrate into the pot– seasoning the cast iron and bringing it back to usefulness.[2]

As I was watching this video, I was struck by how perfectly this depicted the process of transformation that we go through on our spiritual journey to Glory and I was reminded of the passage of Scripture that was chosen for today.

Paul writes to Timothy of the difference between vessels of honor and vessels of dishonor. Those of us who belong to the Lord are to be cleansed of those things that keep us from being used for honor, for every good work, in His kingdom. He goes on to describe those things that we are to avoid, and those things that we are to pursue.

An honorable vessel results from the continuous pursuit of righteousness, faith, love, and peace. We are to avoid quarrels, and be kind, patient, gentle. I think it's important to note that these qualities, this transformation from dishonor to honor, is Holy Spirit generated, but it comes when we are yielded and surrendered to God. Our part in the cleansing process is to be willing for Him to show us those behaviors and qualities that are not honorable, not righteous, and then to ask Him for the mercy and grace to change.

Many times this process occurs in our lives as we are refined through the fires of difficulty. Just as that old cast iron pot yields to the heat and expands to allow that seasoning process to work, the fires of trials can be the tools that the Lord uses to season us, to transform us, to sanctify, or set us apart, for His work, as we allow the Holy Spirit to penetrate deep into our being.

Be sure that this process is not to make us into a museum piece that sits on a shelf or in a case, never to be touched or used. No, we are meant to be instruments of grace and honor in service to our great King. The more we are used in His service, the more His Holy Spirit pervades our lives, transforming us from glory-to-glory.

Brenda says of her cast iron pot, if you want to make it better, "Cook in it!"

Likewise, if we want to see the transformation in our lives that the Holy Spirit can bring about, we must say to Him, "Use me."

If you are struggling with sin in your life today, if your desire is to be used for honor in God's kingdom, ask the Lord for the grace to be cleansed. Yield to His cleansing and transforming power.

Maybe you feel that you can never become that vessel of honor you desire to be. Don't give up hope.

Keep pursuing those things that please the Lord and He will fulfill His promise that you "will be a vessel for honor, sanctified, useful to the Master, prepared for every good work" (v. 21).

December 3

Ninety-two Bananas

Psalm 138

Today I want to share with you the story of a woman named Darlene Diebler Rose, a missionary in the jungles of New Guinea during World War II who was captured and survived four years in a Japanese prison camp.

During her time in the prison camp, Darlene maintained a strong faith and determination to survive and keep her testimony of the Lord's goodness and salvation strong. She had many encounters with the notorious camp commander, Mr. Yamaji, who was well known for his violent temper and who was physically abusive to Darlene and the others in the camp, some to the point of severe injury and even death.

On the day Darlene was told her husband had died earlier in another camp, Mr. Yamaji called her to his office. With uncharacteristic sympathy, the commander encouraged Darlene not to allow her grief to cause her to lose hope because her leadership and temperament was a great help to the other women in the camp. He tried to comfort her by telling her that she was not alone in her grief as others had also experienced loss. Darlene saw this conversation as an opportunity that she might never get again. She asked permission to speak to him, and he gestured to her to sit.

Darlene told him, "Mr. Yamaji, I don't sorrow like people who have no hope. I want to tell you about Someone of Whom you may never have heard…. His name is Jesus. He's the Son of Almighty God, the Creator of heaven and earth….He died for you, Mr Yamaji, and he puts love in our hearts– even for those who are our enemies…. Maybe God brought me to this place and this time to tell you He loves you." At that, Mr. Yamaji stood and walked out of the office, tears streaming down his face, and went into his adjoining bedroom.

In May of 1944, Darlene was taken from the camp to a prison that had formerly been an insane asylum. She was charged with spying and sentenced to death. Day after day she was physically and mentally tortured, and nearly starved. Despite the horrible conditions, she sang hymns in her cell, and recited Bible verses she had memorized. Still she grew so weak it was difficult for her to stand. When the guards came to her cell door she was expected to stand and bow to show respect. Even this simple effort was nearly impossible for her as she was so physically weakened.

One day, Darlene was watching from her window as women from another cell block were outside. One particular woman caught her attention, as she ventured closer and closer to a fence that was overgrown with shrubs. Darlene suspected there was someone on the other side of the shrubs, and she was right. Soon the prisoner quickly reached into the shrubs, and before the guard could see, hid a bunch of bananas in the folds of her skirt.

Darlene couldn't stop thinking of those bananas! She even prayed for God to send her just one. But she knew that there was no one who would bring her a banana. Even the kindest of the guards would likely be shot if he were caught doing such a thing.

The next morning, she heard footsteps approaching her door. Darlene summoned all her strength to stand and prepared to bow to whoever was on the other side of the door. When the door was opened, there stood Mr. Yamaji. She greeted him as if he were an old friend, but was shocked when tears filled his eyes and he turned and walked away without a word. Soon, he came back. He said to her, "You're very ill, aren't you?" Darlene replied, "Yes, sir. I am." After she gave him a message to send back to the women at the camp, he left again.

When Darlene heard the guard's footsteps returning, she was fearful, remembering that she had failed to bow when they had come back with Mr. Yamaji. She didn't think she could endure another beating. But when the door opened, the guard, in a sweeping motion laid at her feet a large bunch of bananas. Stunned, Darlene sat down and counted– there were ninety-two of them![3]

How the Lord longs to bless us! How He loves to hear our prayers and our praise. We belong to a God Who is exalted and magnified, a God Who is never limited by our circumstances. He hears the cries of even the lowliest of His children.

Perhaps today you are feeling overwhelmed, or even forgotten.

Use today's Psalm as your prayer, and remember

that the Lord's lovingkindness is everlasting.

He will save you, He will never forsake you, and

He will accomplish that which concerns you.

December 4

Desperate Faith: The Woman with the Issue

Mark 5:25-34

Written by: Debi Hutchens

In 2006, I underwent an unexpected open heart surgery that seemed to open-up a Pandora's Box of uncertainties, complications, another hidden diagnosis, a plethora of new specialists, and a reckless desperation to find healing or some aspect of it. Donning the label of disabled and fervently trying to figure out what that even meant. One of my friends told me in jest the more "ologists" one has, the shorter their life span—so according to her thinking, I am definitely in trouble after adding a surplus of medical professionals over the years to my story.

During my pursuit for answers to my newfound affliction, I met this woman with a desperate faith despite the odds against her—a nameless woman. A woman legally branded under Jewish law as "unclean" because of an issue of blood. Unable to go into the temple for religious ceremonies. Others fearful of being near her, afraid they too might be labeled dirty if they happened to touch her. The woman facing the risk of certain death if she did not follow the Jewish protocol of "the unclean." Isolated—Alone—Wretched—Miserable—

and most definitely, Spent.

Known in the Bible only as a "certain" woman, she toted her heavy baggage of this issue daily for twelve years all alone. She was tired—broken physically, spiritually, and monetarily as she hopelessly sought for her deliverance from this curse. Day-by-day, her condition was growing worse, but having already exhausted every other resource and treatment available, she was running out of options. Definitely nowhere else to turn after looking for healing in all the "wrong" places. But then she heard about Jesus' healing power—pondering if only she could touch the hem of the Great Physician's garment she would be made whole again and would no longer be shunned because she was considered filthy.

She was also a woman with a definite mission. Imagine the moment as she entered the immense crowd pressing persistently around Jesus. Frantically searching for the One who could end her sickness as she intently pushed herself through the horde to get closer to Jesus. Steadfast to not let the thick crowd stop her, realizing that those she bumped into could become unclean as well, but she pressed on.

Immediately as she touched the Hope of all hope, her issue was totally gone. After years of suffering, she was completely healed! Although hard-pressed on every side by the crowd that sought Him, Jesus felt her touch and asked the disciples, "Who touched my clothes?" No doubt, He already knew all about her, but stopped amid the crowd to acknowledge this one who sought Him sincerely.

Ponder as this certain woman humbly falls down at His feet, trembling with awe, in view of the very people who avoided her because she once was unclean. Envision the first time she recognizes her Savior and what He had done in her life—where man had failed, Jesus triumphed.

I can only imagine His compassionate eyes looking down at her and thinking, "This is my beloved daughter in whom I am well pleased. Her faith has made her whole."

Moreover, this is my prayer—please

let my faith be desperate enough to make me

wholeheartedly seek Him—and to be able to

look into His compassionate eyes.

December 5

What Are You Looking For?

2 Peter 3:8-15

I'm not going to lie– I have used Pandemic 2020 as an excuse to spend a lot more money than I should have. I did not hoard toilet paper or cleaning products or Le Sueur Very Young Small Sweet Peas like some of you did, though. Oh, but I have bought some things– so much that I can now identify UPS, FedEx, and the Post Man solely by the sound of their trucks. In December of 2019, I toyed with the idea of not renewing my Amazon Prime membership. By March, I had never been happier to pay that $119!

Watching the shelves empty at the stores gave us a glimpse of what people are finding to provide comfort and security. We are seeing an almost intense reliance on having things that are the most basic of necessities.

We have seen our country open up a little at a time. We have seen that curve flatten, then rise as people became less consistent with pandemic practices and more determined to get life back to normal. Today, as I'm writing this in the heat of summer, the uncertainty about the virus remains strong, but the desire for normalcy is heavy in all our hearts. We are weary of living under the shadow of COVID-19.

Our attention is strongly on the numbers. When will it end? When can we visit our families and friends? When can we put the masks away? As the weeks and months continue with seemingly no end in sight, we desperately want to hear good news.

Time continues the rapid march toward Christmas, bringing us to this precious time of Advent. Reminding us that our eyes must be fixed far beyond the end of the Pandemic and that our attention must stay even more firmly planted toward Christ's second Advent. This was the reminder that the Apostle Peter brought to the persecuted believers from Rome who had been scattered throughout the region of what is now Turkey.

His encouragement: The greatest hope for all mankind for all history is the hope of Heaven where we will live redeemed and transformed in the presence of our Father. Peter reminds us that one day this earth will melt away and a new earth, in which righteousness dwells, will take its place.

When will it happen? When will the interminable days of suffering and loss end? Peter encouraged us in verse 8 not to confuse the Lord's patience with slowness. His lovingkindness and mercy are why He tarries– wanting all to come to repentance, because those who don't will perish.

Therefore, we wait– and as we wait, we "hasten" His coming. The hastening Peter uses here means that we are eagerly waiting for it. We are looking for the coming of the day of God (our eternal state in Heaven). Three times Peter uses that phrase looking for, but not in a sense that we are merely standing around gazing at the sky.

Looking for means that we are living lives worthy of the redemption we've been given. Verse 11 describes it as "holy conduct and godliness." Second, verse 13 tells us that looking for involves living in faith– believing "according to His promise." And finally, verse 14 shows us how we are being transformed as we look for these things– that we are diligent about being at peace, and about being spotless and blameless.

You may find it difficult to read Peter's words about the earth and heavens melting with the intense heat of the judgement of God. You may question the goodness of a God Who would threaten to thoroughly destroy the creation He is supposed to love.

I believe that since man's sinful Fall back in the Garden, this has always been part of God's plan to fully transform the entire Creation back to the glory He had intended for us. This dramatic ending is also the glorious beginning. God's plans are not meant to cause God's children to fear, but to give us great hope and to impact the way that we live.

As we feel the weariness of living through days of fear, anger, violence, and uncertainty, this promise gives us great peace. We are at peace knowing that these fearful days will one day be over. This peace is not just reserved for a future time, but can be experienced right now in the midst of the chaos.

Maybe today your heart can't seem to find this peace– your heart is bound in fear and turmoil. Maybe the thought of Christ's return doesn't fill you with great joy and anticipation, but just more worry and anguish. If that's the case, then God's patience is meant for you. He has paused the eternal destiny of all of mankind to wait for you to come to Him in repentance. What mercy and kindness He has for you.

What greater time than this Advent season to begin looking for– and finding– your Savior.

December 6

An Advent Prayer

God of timeless grace,

You fill us with joyful expectation.

Make us ready for the message that

prepares the way,

That with uprightness of heart and holy joy

We may eagerly await the kingdom of

Your Son, Jesus Christ,

Who reigns with You and the Holy Spirit,

now and forever. Amen.

God of hope

You raised up John the baptizer

As a herald who calls us to conversion.

As we joyfully await the glorious coming of Christ

We pray to You for the needs of

the church and the world.

Hear our humble prayer,

That we may serve You in holiness and faith

And give voice to Your presence among us

Until the day of the coming of

Your Son, Jesus Christ

Who lives and reigns for ever and ever. Amen.

God of hope,

You call us from the exile of our sin

With the good news of restoration;

You build a highway through the wilderness;

You come to us and bring us home.

Comfort us with the expectation of

Your saving power,

Made known to us in Jesus Christ our Lord.

Amen.[4]

December 7

Rescued, Revived, Rejoicing

Psalm 85

The late Ravi Zacharias shared the story of an interpreter who worked with him during his ministry in Vietnam in 1971– a young, energetic believer named Hien Pham. Hien also worked as a translator with the American forces, so shortly after Vietnam fell in 1975, Hien was arrested on accusations of helping the Americans.

During his time of imprisonment, he was forced to read only communist propaganda. Day after day, his jailers tried to indoctrinate him against his Christian belief, and eventually his mind and his heart were so saturated, he began to give in to doubt. One day he thought maybe he had been wrong about God– perhaps he had been deceived by the American missionaries. He determined that the next day he would not pray anymore or think of his faith. Ravi writes:

The next morning, Hien was assigned the dreaded chore of cleaning the prison latrines. As he cleaned out a tin can over-flowing with toilet paper, his eye caught what seemed to be English printed on one piece of paper. He hurriedly grabbed it, washed it, and after his roommates had retired that night, he retrieved the paper and read the words, "Romans, Chapter 8." Trembling, he began to read, "And we know that in all things God works for the good of those who love him, who have been called according to his purpose...For I am convinced that neither death nor life, neither angels nor demons, neither the present nor the future, nor any power, neither height nor depth, nor anything else in all creation, will be able to separate us from the love of God that is in Christ Jesus our Lord.

Hien wept. He knew his Bible, and he knew that there was not a more relevant passage for one on the verge of surrender. He cried out to God asking for forgiveness. This was to have been the first day he would not pray; evidently, God had other plans.

As it were, there was an official in the camp who was using a Bible as toilet paper. So Hien asked the commander if he could clean the latrines regularly. Each day he picked up a portion of Scripture, cleaned it off, and added it to his collection of nightly reading.[5]

God Himself rescued and revived Hien's dwindling faith. In the middle of an all-out attack against all that he believed, God's truth literally sprang from the earth (Psalm 85:11) to accomplish God's restoration of this man's hope. In His sovereignty, God indeed worked "all things for good." He brought Hien to a place where His faith was tested, so that out of the clouds that darkened his hope, God could show Himself unquestionably faithful in His lovingkindness and in His ability to save.

You may look at that situation and think that because of the dire circumstances Hien was in that God had to resort to such a miracle. You may think that God doesn't pursue us in our normal, often mundane lives. I want to share with you my friend Tonya's story, as she told it to me, and encourage you that God has many instruments at His disposal to use to bring us back to Him.

I had fallen away from church when I left home to join the Air Force. I have always believed, but wasn't accountable to live the way He would have me to live. I was told for over ten years that I would never have children— and I had accepted it. My prayer was— "if it is Your will, there will be a way." The Lord saw fit for me to be a mom, and blessed me with Nick. I gave Him the praise, but I still didn't go to church. Co-workers had been inviting me to church, but I kept putting them off.

When Nick was 18-months old I was tucking him into bed and turned to leave the room. He sat up and said, "When I was a baby Jesus used to rock me in His arms like this..." and he made a rocking motion with his arms. This baby was 18-months old. He had never been to church.

I turned around and dropped to my knees next to his bed and prayed. I was transformed. I couldn't believe that the Lord had pursued me the way He had. He had blessed me with a child– who was I not to raise him up in God's ways?

That was a Tuesday night. I went to work the next morning and asked my friend where her church was located and what time the Wednesday night service started. That next service, I was there with my son.

God rescued me, He redeemed me, and He is still working to transform me. I'm a work in progress.

My son accepted the Lord at age 5 and was baptized at age 6. He's now 21 and still comes to me to ask me to pray for him when he is carrying a burden.

In these days when belief can be hard, when our faith is constantly challenged, questioned, and even belittled, God's promise for us is simple. It is the promise of a kingdom of lovingkindness and truth and righteousness and peace. It is the promise that "Indeed, the Lord will give what is good, and our land will yield its produce." It is the promise that His salvation is near to those who fear Him, that His glory will dwell in our land (verses 10-12).

If today your faith is being tested, or if, like Tonya, you are not living close to the Lord, rest on these great promises of God. Yes, He will, Himself, revive us again so that we may rejoice in Him.

December 8

Open Up the Heavens

Isaiah 64:1-8

Written by: Traci Powell

God's people were in a desperate situation. It seemed that no one was calling on His name and that God had hidden His face. They needed a word from God, they needed to see Him working in a mighty way; they needed rescue, restoration and transformation! Isaiah was crying out for someone to tear open the heavens and come down: To make the mountains quake and to burn like a fire and make his enemies tremble at the power, majesty and might of God!

In the midst of this desperation, Isaiah reminds himself and others of the awesome things that God has done in the past to make Himself known (vv.3-4). God had done awesome things that they did not expect. The mountains even quaked at His presence. God acts on behalf of those who wait for/ trust in Him.

And then as Isaiah remembers who God is, he recognizes his sin and the sins of God's people that deserve punishment. All have sinned and their righteous deeds are like filthy garments (v. 6). He recognizes that no one seeks God or calls on His name on their own.

And finally, he acknowledges that God is our Father. He is the potter, and we are the clay. We are the work of His hand.

Today, we find ourselves in a desperate situation. It seems that not many are calling on His name and that God has hidden His face. We need a word from God, we need to see Him working in a mighty way; we need rescue, restoration and transformation. We would like Him to just tear open the sky and come down.

In reality, there has already been one answer to that cry and there is still one to come. On the day Jesus was baptized (Mark 1:10-11) the heavens were torn open and the Spirit, like a dove, descended on Jesus and God declared that Jesus was His son and that He was pleased with Him. He opened the heavens to declare that the Messiah had come. Our rescuer had come to live the life we could not and die for our sins and bring us to God: redeem us. The ultimate fulfilment of the cry for God to open the heavens will be when Christ returns (Rev. 19:11-16). He will then bring with Him the wrath of God and will wage war with the nations and will exact the final judgement on all those who oppose Him.

Our God has shown us His power with His deeds of the past and declares His power and victory in the future. And we, as His children, should continue to stay close to Him and clean before Him. We know that even though we might not see Him working, He is working. "... God...acts in behalf of the one who waits for Him." God, "You meet him who rejoices in doing righteousness, who remembers You in your ways..." (Isaiah 64: 4b-5a). We must wait for Him, realizing that we can do nothing without Him. No matter how bad it gets, we are His and He is working in and through our lives for His Glory and our good, molding us to be more like Him. He is transforming us. And He uses the very adversity that we hate to bring us back to Himself and to remind us of our dependence on Him.

We have been born into this time in history for a specific reason and with the purpose of glorifying God. Let's call on God, remember what He has done for us in the past, repent of any sins that He brings to mind and willingly cooperate with Him as He molds us and shapes us into what He wants us to be. Ephesians 2:10 tells us, "For we are His workmanship, created in Christ Jesus for good works, which God prepared beforehand so that we would walk in them."

And one day, He will split the sky and

mountains will quake and every eye will see

Him and every knee will bow before Him

and declare that He is Lord of all!

December 9

Which Way the Road Goes

Isaiah 40:1-11, 35:8-10; John 14:1-7

There is nothing better than taking a drive through the farmland of southern middle Georgia on a beautiful day. During the summer, the crepe myrtles line the highways in a parade of blooms that that resonate with everyone who passes by. In the fall, the cotton adorns the fields in what we call Southern Snow. The cattle farms, the Mennonite houses with their wash hung in the front yard, the dirt roads that will take you to secret fishing spots off the river or creek– it's the same road, yet changing with the passing seasons and lingering years.

Have you ever stopped to think about all the roads you know? How you know places and towns by the roads that wind through them? Knowing the road to various places gives you a sense of connection. It gives you a sense of belonging. It gives you a sense of security. And it also reminds you that you know the way to get home.

Isaiah wrote about clearing the road for the Lord in the wilderness. His words, "Make smooth in the desert a highway for our God. Let every valley be lifted up, and every mountain and hill be made low. And let the rough ground become a plain, and the rugged terrain a broad valley. Then the glory of the Lord will be revealed, and all flesh will see it together."

Earlier, Isaiah had also mentioned that highway when he wrote,

"A highway will be there, a roadway, and it will be called the Highway of Holiness. The unclean will not travel on it, but it will be for him who walks that way, and fools will not wander on it....But the redeemed will walk there, and the ransomed of the Lord will return and come with joyful shouting to Zion, with everlasting joy upon their heads. They will find gladness and joy, and sorrow and sighing will flee away." Isaiah 35:8-10

The prophet, and later John the Baptist who quoted Isaiah, tell us to make a smooth highway for our God. In other words, we are to prepare ourselves for His return. We do that through first trusting Jesus for our salvation. Through repentance, or turning away from our sinful ways, and then through steady obedience to His transforming work in our lives.

But none of these things rely only on us. Yes, we must believe. And yes, we must surrender to Him. But I love how Isaiah ends this passage. He writes, "Behold, the Lord God will come with might, with His arm ruling for Him.... Like a shepherd He will tend His flock, in His arms He will gather the lambs and carry them in His bosom. He will gently lead the nursing ewes."

The picture of Jesus being born in a stable, laid in a manger as a newborn, reminds us that He is our shepherd. That He will lovingly gather His lambs, He will carry us in his bosom– that place of protection that is close to His own heart.

The picture of the Lord God coming in His might reminds us that He will one day soon return with great power to defeat His enemies. What glorious promises these are for all of us who believe.

I don't know about you, but I long for the eternal joy and gladness that God's Word promises. I long for the time when all sorrow and sighing will be gone.

There is such a wonderful sense of security, peace, comfort, and belonging to know that we can know the way to Heaven. Maybe today you are not sure if you're on the right road– the road that leads to glory. Even one of Jesus's own disciples asked Him, "Lord, we do not know where You are going, how do we know the way?" Jesus' answer to that disciple, and to us, is very simple, "I am the way, and the truth, and the life."

There are a lot of choices in this world– ideas or philosophies to believe in, politicians or leaders to follow– a lot of roads are being opened up. But there is only one road that leads to Heaven– and that is the road that Jesus is on. Make sure today that you are on that road, and that road only.

Let this loving Shepherd gather you in His arms

and carry you close to His heart until

He comes to take us to Glory.

December 10

A Sip of Living Water

Psalm 46 and Revelation 22:1-5

On November 14, 1992, Vietnam Airlines Flight 474 crashed into the thick jungle on a remote mountainside. Some of the passengers survived the initial crash, only to perish from their injuries before they could be rescued. After eight days, rescuers were finally able to locate the crash site and discovered only one survivor among the wreckage.

Annette Herfkens is a Dutch business woman from New York who was on vacation with her fiancé. Having survived the crash, she was unable to move because of her injuries, which included both hips being shattered. For eight days she laid in the jungle, among the decaying bodies of her fiancé and the rest of the passengers and crew, surviving only on whatever drops of rainwater she could manage to swallow from sponges she fashioned from the plane's insulation.

Finally, a rescue team located her. As one of the men approached her, he held out a container of fresh water. In recounting this in an interview she said, "I will never forget that first sip of water."[6]

God's people have the unfailing promise of rescue to hold onto. When we take our first step of faith in trusting in Jesus Christ, we receive that first sip of living water. This water cleanses us of our unrighteousness so that through Christ we can be rescued from eternal separation from God.

This water refreshes us during our most spiritually dry and thirsty days so that we are sustained here on earth through countless hardships and heartaches.

The image in Psalms 46:4-5 is both beautiful and comforting. "There is a river whose streams make glad the city of God. The holy dwelling places of the Most High. God is in the midst of her, she will not be moved; God will help her when morning dawns."

Revelation 22:1 tells us more: "Then he showed me a river of the water of life, clear as crystal, coming from the throne of God and of the Lamb." In his commentary on this passage, John MacArthur writes: "This river is unlike any on earth because no hydrological cycle exists. Water of life symbolizes the continual flow of eternal life from God's throne to heaven's inhabitants." (MacArthur, 2006, p. 1995)

When Jesus rescues us, when He gives us that first sip of His living water, we are forever changed. We become partakers in His promise that we can dwell in His eternal kingdom— that place where there will no longer be any curse, no longer be any right, and we will serve and reign with Him, face to face with Him, forever and ever (Rev. 22:3-5).

Mankind is thirsty— we are parched, and trying to survive on droplets of water that, though the best the world has to offer, is still contaminated. Before Him, we have sought so many ways to quench our thirst. But instead of being satisfied, we have ended up being more and more thirsty. Nothing this world offers compares— not wealth, not power, not fame. Only the living water that comes from Christ.

When Christ stepped down from His throne in Heaven to live on earth among men, He brought with Him this Living Water for all who thirst. He pours this out for us, freely, generously, with great mercy and compassion— rescuing us from our jungle of sin, insecurity, and brokenness.

During this Advent season, may you experience
the gladness of this living water, and
know its transforming power in your life.

December 11

Looking Forward to Glory

2 Corinthians 4:16-18

Written by: Dr. David Grantham

The world has become so me focused in today's culture. There seems to be a huge desire to accumulate personal things and to climb the ladder of the worldly success system. Because people do not want to endanger their pathway to success, they tend to go along with the crowd so as to assure themselves of worldly success. As believers, we must be willing to stand up for the Word of God which typically means that we will face persecution.

No one desires to be persecuted in life, but as Followers of Christ, we must expect persecution to be a part of our lives. Jesus tells us in John 15:18-20, "If the world hates you, you know that it hated Me before it hated you. If you were of the world, the world would love its own. Yet because you are not of the world, but I chose you out of the world, therefore the world hates you. Remember the word that I said to you, A servant is not greater than his master. If they persecuted Me, they will also persecute you. If they kept My word, they will keep yours also." Jesus plainly instructs His followers that they will endure persecution and affliction as a result of following Him.

The Apostle Paul was one such follower. After Paul had his Damascus Road experience in Acts chapter nine, he began preaching Christ to the Jews. Paul faced many afflictions as a result of preaching the gospel of Christ. He was stoned, beaten with rods three times, shipwrecked, and imprisoned on several occasions.

How could Paul endure all the trials and afflictions he faced? Paul endured his persecution because his focus was on a future glory. Paul had had an encounter with the risen Savior. Paul knew the glory of God was more significant than his earthly affliction. Paul did not have his eyes looking at the outward man, but he kept his eyes on the inward man.

Paul was locked in on the glory of what was yet to come. Author Philip Hughes concludes, "Affliction for Jesus' sake, however crushing it might seem, is in fact light, a weightless trifle, when weighed against the mass of that glory."[7] Everyday Paul's spiritual, inner man was getting stronger and stronger. Paul's body was marked by the outward decay of growing old and the trials of this world, but Paul's inner man was maturing and becoming an impenetrable fortress.

Today followers of Christ must be able to navigate our journeys in life facing persecution head on and rejoicing that we have been chosen to receive trials. The apostles went from being afraid of persecution while Jesus was physically alive to rejoicing in persecution after the Holy Spirit was given to them after the resurrection.

The apostles were preaching in the temple and got arrested by the religious leaders. The religious leaders had mixed opinions of what to do with the apostles, but Gamaliel convinces them to release them. Acts 5:40-42 says, "And they agreed with him, and when they had called for the apostles and beaten them, they commanded that they should not speak in the name of Jesus, and let them go. So they departed from the presence of the council, rejoicing that they were counted worthy to suffer shame for His name."

The apostles finally grasped what Jesus had been teaching them throughout His three-year training process. The apostles were to no longer fear what man could do to them, but to fear Him who can kill both body and soul (Matthew 10:28). We need to have a reverent awe of the glory of God.

One day we will see His face and His glory will be revealed. That will be a magical day. We will never be separated from His presence again! Hallelujah.

December 12

What Are You Wearing?

Isaiah 61:10-11, Matthew 22:11-14

I am one of the most socially awkward people in the world. If you've ever gotten stuck in an endless loop of "Fine, how are you?" ...it was with me. I have been known to have committed some social blunders that still keep me up at night! However, the man in Jesus' parable in the book of Matthew committed more than just a fashion faux pas.

In Matthew 22 we read about a king who gave a great wedding feast for his son. When the people who were initially invited to the feast ignored the invitation, the king sent his servants out to invite anyone and everyone– both evil and good– and the wedding hall was filled! During the feast, the king noticed a guest who was not dressed in wedding clothes. When the king confronted him, the guest was speechless– he had no excuse. So the king had the man thrown into the "outer darkness– in that place there will be weeping and gnashing of teeth."

Let's take a quick look at the cast of characters. There is the king and His Son. They represent God the Father and Jesus Christ. Then there are the original invitees who refused (some violently) the invitation to the feast. They represent the Jewish people who rejected the Messiah. The servants represent the prophets who God sent to the Jewish people.

Then there is the general population of people who accepted the invitation. Those people are the non-Jewish people who have accepted Jesus as Messiah, as Lord. And then there's this guy. Who is he?

We know he wasn't wearing the wedding garment. Now, this was not an issue of the guest not having the right clothes to wear. It was customary for wedding guests to be given special clothes to wear for the wedding feast; so clearly, the guest merely refused to wear the clothes that the king had made available. By coming in his own clothes, even if he was wearing his very best suit, he was essentially refusing the one thing the king required of his guests. And the one thing the king required, the king himself provided.

The man who showed up at the wedding feast without the wedding clothes thought he belonged. He had been invited. He showed up. Look at all the other people who were also invited and showed up. Like them, the guest was taking advantage of the gracious invitation of the king. He just erroneously thought his own clothes were good enough.

Back to the question, Who is he? This man is every person who has ever tried to earn their way to Heaven on their own merit. He is the person who thinks that church attendance, or singing in the choir, or being baptized will pave His way to eternity in Heaven.

He is the one who is a good person, who volunteers, who is a faithful spouse and an attentive parent. But those are just the clothes he puts on every morning. Inside, he is lost because he has refused the garments provided by the Father. He is exhausted and defeated trying to reach a standard by his own efforts that he can't even begin to reach.

Isaiah describes for us the garments of salvation and robes of righteousness. Notice that those garments are given to us by God, and that He gives them freely. I love the picture of God wrapping me up in a robe of righteousness, taking my ugly, tattered, sin-soaked garments away, and replacing them with a clean, spotless robe that he lovingly covers me with.

He gives these clothes to all who recognize that their own righteousness is not good enough, and who come to Him with a heart ready to accept God's mercy and grace. This is why Jesus came and why He died– so that His perfect blood would cover my sin, so that God could cloak me in the righteousness of the perfect and precious Savior.

I have come to understand that a lot of people have ideas about salvation that are completely their own personal concoctions– ideas that have no Scriptural backing whatsoever. This is too important a question for conjecture or debate. The Bible clearly tells us that there is only one way to Heaven, and that way is Jesus.

The question for you today is, what are you wearing? Are you clothed in garments of salvation, robes of righteousness, given to you by God Himself? Or are you hoping to get into Heaven in garments you've made for yourself?

Pray today that God will help you to see

exactly where you stand with Him. If you are

wearing your own good works, ask Him for

those garments of salvation that He

has made just for you.

December 13

An Advent Prayer

The Miracle: Exodus 14

God of hope

You call us home from the exile

of selfish oppression

To the freedom of justice,

The balm of healing,

And the joy of sharing.

Make us strong to join you in your holy work,

As friends of strangers and victims

Companions of those whom others shun

And as the happiness of those

whose hearts are broken.

Brothers and sisters,

As we joyfully await the glorious coming of Christ

Let us pray for the needs of the church,

our community, and the world.

God of joy and exultation,

You strengthen what is weak

You enrich the poor,

And give hope to those who live in fear.

Look upon our needs this day

Make us grateful for the good news of salvation

And keep us faithful in Your service

Until the coming of our Lord Jesus Christ

Who lives for ever and ever. Amen.

Merciful God of peace

Your work, spoken by the prophets

Restores your people's life and hope.

Fill our hearts with the joy of your saving grace

That we may hold fast to your great goodness

And in our lives proclaim your justice

in all the world. Amen.[4]

December 14

Help My Unbelief

Mark 9:14-23

In today's passage is the account of a man who brings his demon-possessed son to Jesus to be healed. Since childhood, the boy had been plagued by a demon who made him mute, and even tried to destroy him with fire and water. We are not told how many years had transpired– it's a detail that doesn't matter. Even one episode of such violence is more than enough for a father to witness his child experience. All we know is that the boy was "often" thrown into the water and the fire by this destructive demon.

How many doctors had the man taken the boy to? How many holy men? How many therapies, how many prayers, how many vows and offerings and sacrifices had been made?

Finally, he hears of this man Jesus who is healing the multitudes. Even Jesus' disciples have the power to heal. Once again, the man's hope is stirred up for his son to be healed.

He brings the boy to the disciples, only to see their efforts fail. Again he walks away disappointed.

But then, the man brings the boy directly to Jesus. What can it hurt? Maybe it will help him.

The man tells Jesus, "If you can do anything, take pity on us and help us!"

If I pause there, one word that stands out to me is the word us.

This child was not alone in his battle— it was as much the father's as it was the son's.

Jesus, however, honed in on the phrase, *If you can*. He responded to the father with words of great assurance and compassion— "All things are possible to him who believes."

Jesus knew that He was going to heal this boy. His power was not dependent upon the father's faith. But He saw in the father's heart the weariness that comes from years of hoping and believing in cures that never cured his son. The son's problem was the demon-possession. The father's problem was a faith that was being weakened by the ongoing circumstances— the helpless fear, the anguish of watching his son on the brink of destruction over and over again, compounded by the disappointment of failed attempts at wholeness.

Could the father identify his own problem as well as he could identify his son's?

Mark tells us that "Immediately the boy's father cried out and said, 'I do believe; help my unbelief."

Jesus did heal the boy, commanding the demon to come out and never enter him again.

But the prayer of the father for Christ to heal his unbelief was a prayer for his condition to be healed for all eternity.

I can identify with the father's "if you can" question. Having lived with an advancing chronic disease for decades I've faced failed treatments, ineffective medications and lifestyle changes that may work for only a short period of time.

I've prayed so often for Jesus to heal me, but he hasn't. And I don't know what to do with that. I don't dare question His power, because I see evidence of His power everywhere I look. I don't dare question His compassion and mercy, because they are visibly new each morning as I'm able to get out of bed and go about my life despite the pain. I cannot question His kindness, His love, or His provision, because He is remarkably generous beyond all I can fathom.

I admit, though, that some days it's hard not to focus on the circumstances that I want God to change in my life. It's hard to keep believing He can when He chooses not to.

Maybe you're at that place in your life as well.

On those days we don't understand why the healing won't come, why the relationship isn't restored, why the money isn't enough despite years of praying and trusting– on the days when belief dwindles, make the prayer of the boy's father your own.

May God rescue us from our unbelief when

circumstances crowd out the truth of His goodness.

May He give us the faith to pray for His will alone

during times we just don't understand.

December 15

Rescue in the Storm

Mark 4:35-41

Written by: Traci Powell

The disciples were in God's will. They had done as Jesus had asked. At Jesus' command they left for the other side of the lake and He went to the back of the boat to sleep.

Then came the storm, not just any storm but a fierce tempest with driving wind and rain. The waves were breaking over the boat and it was filling with water! Terrifying!

Jesus was not disturbed at all– He slept on.

They woke Him in a panic, wondering if He even cared that they were about to die. He rebuked the storm with three little words: Quiet, be still. The storm obeyed immediately and became calm. Then He rebuked the disciples for their lack of faith. The disciples were in awe and they became very much afraid and marveled that even the wind and sea obeyed Him.

We may be in the middle of God's will– or not– and the chaos around us can seem like a wild storm that no one can stop. There is no rescue. God seems silent: Is He asleep? Will we all perish? My circumstances are threatening to drown me! Does He even care?

He knows exactly what He is allowing in your life and exactly what He can do with that circumstance or problem or person to grow you and make you more like Him. There is something that needs to be accomplished in your life with this storm.

Do you need a Word from Him? Go to the Words that He has already spoken, the promises that He has already made, and spend time "hearing" what the Lord has to say to you. Go to His Word to find comfort, peace, strength, hope; all that you need for the storm. The rescue comes in the words of our Master. As we look to Him, His words may still the storm or just still our hearts. But we can be sure He will rescue us!

Our rescue can come in many ways:

He could still the storm and show His power

He could steer you around the storm and show His wisdom

He could take you through the storm and show His peace

He could take you out of the storm and show His mercy.

But He is always there. He promised that He would never leave us or forsake us (Hebrews 13:5).

Remember that anything God allows in our lives has purpose. It can be used for our good and His glory—to make His name known.

Let us not hear the rebuke that Jesus gave the disciples "Why are you so afraid? Do you still have not faith?" rather "Trust in the Lord with all your heart and lean not on your own understanding, in all your ways acknowledge Him and He will make your paths straight." Prov. 3:5-6

We, like the disciples, should worship Him in reverence and awe when we realize that "even the winds and the waves obey Him"! Trust Him who has all the power and the glory and the honor forever!

December 16

Can You Thank Me?

Romans 8:18-30

For I consider that the sufferings of this present time are not worthy to be compared with the glory that is to be revealed in us. (v. 18)

I remember Dr. Helen Roseveare from her visit to Toccoa Falls College during my days as a student there. She came during one of the weeks that we called "spiritual emphasis" as guest speaker. She wasn't dynamic in her appearance or demeanor, and her voice, with her British accent, wasn't one I remember as particularly demanding. But there was a quality about her that made me want to hear what she had to say. I suppose the word to describe her would be compelling.

In college, most often the "doctors" who took the pulpit were PhD's. But Dr. Roseveare was a medical doctor– a former missionary in central Africa. She had served in the Congo during the rebel uprising in the 1960's, and endured discrimination, distrust and suspicion among the people she was serving, as well as the typical difficulties of running a teaching hospital and seminary in the heat of the jungle.

In her books chronicling the years of her ministry, she shows how each obstacle she encountered, each difficulty she endured, was a moment for God to change her, refine her, and show His love to her and to the people He sent her to serve.

In October of 1964, Dr. Roseveare and the two nurses who were staying in her home were awakened to soldiers who swarmed through the house throwing books and dishes on the floor. Most of the soldiers then left, presumably not finding what they were searching for. But the head lieutenant called some of them back and ordered the doctor back into the house.

As they beat her, kicked her, and raped her, she writes, "*It was as if (God) spoke to me: 'Can you thank Me...' and every ounce of my energy wanted to scream out, 'No!' How could I thank Him for this wickedness and evil? But His quiet voice went on: 'Can you thank Me for trusting you...'*

That was an amazing thought! For me to trust Him, yes, I knew that; but for Him to trust me was a fantastic turn of the situation. Was He saying to me, 'Yes I could have kept you out of this situation: I could have rescued you... but I thought I could trust you to go through this with Me, as I have a plan and purpose for the future'?

Again: 'Can you thank Me for trusting you with this experience even if I never tell you why?' Somehow, in the darkness of that appalling night, I managed to say to my dear Lord, 'I don't understand what You may be doing, or who can be helped through this ordeal (I was certain we would all be killed), but, yes, if You ask this of me, thank You for trusting me with this experience even if You never tell me why.'

Immediately, I knew that He was with me, that He knew what was happening, and that He knew how this could help forward His plan in future days. Yes, the pain was still there– He did not take away the evil, the shame, the pain– but so too was an overwhelming sense of

His peace, His presence, His love.[9]

There will be a point in the life of every child of God where we will have that same conversation with Him. Perhaps you are having that conversation with Him in whatever you are facing in your life now. It is a conversation from the midst of the unthinkable, that ends in our utter surrender to Him. In that moment when we have that overwhelming sense of His presence with us in our suffering, we are able to understand in the depth of our souls just how trustworthy our Savior is.

It is that complete surrender to Him that transforms us. It sharpens our understanding of where our hope is found. It fills us with peace that can't be explained. It brings us deeper into fellowship with Christ. It places us fully into the power of living according to His will. It conforms us to the image of God's Son. It frees us to enjoy the glory God has for His children. Only He can bring us from suffering to glory.

What is God asking of you today? What suffering is He leading you through right now? Ask Him for the faith and trust to surrender to Him, and for the grace to be grateful to Him even in your trials. He does have a plan and a purpose for all that concerns you. Pray for His peace, His presence, and His love to overwhelm you as you settle your life into His hands.

As you meditate on the Advent Scripture

today, may your heart be encouraged by the

glory that is yet to come.

December 17

Spark of Life

2 Corinthians 3:18-4:6

There is a remarkable thing that happens at the moment of human conception. When those two single-cells meet for the first time there is something called a zinc spark. There is literally a small burst of light at the moment of conception which creates a unique halo effect around the now-fertilized egg, signifying that a new little life has begun.[10] Fertility researchers, Teresa Woodruff and Tom O'Halloran, discovered this phenomenon, and called this burst of light nothing short of breathtaking.[11]

You know, I think it's absolutely amazing that God has allowed us to see this incredible bit of biology that once more supports the biblical truth that He has created us in His image, and that He has designed all of us to give evidence to His glory– even from the very moment of conception.

We were designed for glory. We were always intended to be a reflection of the magnificent God Who created us in His image. The Bible tells us that all of creation– including mankind– is made for His glory. Nothing can change this truth, and nothing can extinguish even a little bit the great glory of God. Sin has distorted that image in mankind and can dull our reflection of Him, but all of creation declares God's glory, and nothing can change that.

There is a difference between being designed for glory and being destined for glory. And that difference rests in what we do with Jesus.

Now is a good time to read, or re-read, the passage of Scripture for today. These verses talk about "the light of the gospel of the glory of Christ, who is the image of God." (verse 4)

Paul distinguishes between two groups of people in these verses. One group he describes as "those who are perishing." This is the same type of "perish" that Jesus talked about in John 3:16, and is literally an eternal spiritual death. Everyone is born into a world of spiritual darkness– dark because of the fallen nature of man. And that fallen nature is the result of the work of Satan, who Paul says has "blinded the minds of the unbelieving."

It isn't difficult to see that this is true. Just expose yourself to any type of media whatsoever these days and you will certainly see that our world definitely caters to man's sinful, depraved nature. Even television commercials are profane and vulgar. Moral lines have been blurred, and every virtue– love, charity, kindness, courage– has been redefined to a standard that lines up with Satan's plans for humanity.

No, it isn't difficult to see the truth of this– unless you yourself have had your mind blinded by Satan. There is a powerful antidote for this blindness, and that antidote is light.

The second group of people, then, are those who have seen (that is, believed) the light of the Gospel. Paul tells us that the same God who spoke light into existence when the universe began is the same One who has "shone in our hearts to give the Light of the knowledge of the glory of God in the face of Christ."

With a single Word, our great, almighty God, speaks the light of the gospel into existence, and at the moment of faith, that light shines in every believing heart, rescuing us from the eternal destiny of spiritual darkness in hell. Spiritual eyes are opened to see His glory, and to see the glory He has destined for His children for all eternity.

For those whose earthly lives end without having been rescued from this spiritual blindness, that spark of light that began at conception is snuffed out. But for those who allow themselves to be rescued by the Gospel of Jesus Christ, that light can never be extinguished.

Once you take hold of Jesus, He begins transforming you "from glory to glory." You are the same "you" that He first breathed that spark of life into. But you are eternally changed. We cannot even begin to imagine the glory that is yet to come.

What will you do with Jesus today? Is your mind still blinded to the light of the Gospel? Or are you allowing the power of His light to transform you from glory to glory? Pray today for eyes that see Him clearly and for the faith to embrace all that He has for you.

December 18

Finally Some Good News

Mark 1:14-20

Written by: Rev. Jamie Powell

It seems that the only news that we hear is bad news. We are constantly bombarded by news of disease, disruption, division, disapproval, depravity. We hear of wars and rumors of war. We hear of crime and corruption, etc., etc. It wears us out and wears us down. Good news seems to be nowhere.

2020 has been a different kind of year for millions (even billions) of people here and around the world. It has been a year of national and global pandemic, disruption of normalcy, shut-downs, unemployment, economic upheaval, social disharmony and unrest, rioting, cultural chaos, political warring, and churches not meeting in person, just to name a few issues. There is fear, worry, frustration, anger, distrust, deception, and criticism everywhere. Even worse, and more importantly, people are living distant and alienated from God, living in darkness and death.

The world and time that Jesus came to was also characterized by people living distant from God, living in darkness and death (Matthew 4:12-16). To this world, and even now, Jesus comes and brings the Gospel (Good news) of God to us. This good news rescues, restores, transforms, and gives new life to those who repent and believe in Him and His Gospel. Those who embrace Jesus and the Gospel, they follow Him. They surrender their lives to Him. As a result, they experience the Lord's work in their lives, they go in the right direction, and they become a personal witness of this good news (Jesus/Gospel) to others.

Mark describes Jesus coming to Andrew, Simon, James, and John and what Jesus had to say to them was so important, He came right to where they worked and interrupted their day, their work, and their lives. He spoke to them and called them to a new life, a new pursuit, a new work, and a new destiny. They responded immediately, completely, and wholeheartedly. Their lives were never the same!

The Lord comes to you, right where you are, and calls you to repent, to believe, and to follow Him. What has been and is your response to Him? These first disciples could not live as they were and follow Jesus. Neither can you. If you are going to follow Jesus, there must be repentance, there must be faith, and there must be surrender.

If you are a believer and follower of Jesus, don't be overwhelmed by the bad news of our day. Be overwhelmed and overjoyed with the Good News of God. God has come to you. God has rescued you. God has brought you near to Him. God has given you new life. The Lord Jesus will lead you in the right direction. The Lord will use you in a life mission that really matters, both now and for eternity.

If you are not a believer, Jesus says to you: "Repent and

believe in the Gospel." Change your mind about your

sin, about the direction you are going, and about Jesus.

Believe in Jesus as your Savior and Lord.

Surrender all and follow Him.

December 19

The Lord Has Done Great Things for Us

Psalm 126

Written by: Debi Hutchens

For the past several months, we have been taken captive in a strange, dry–land by an intrusive enemy. An unseen virus that has entangled many in the chains of bondage of the unknown, causing fearfulness, anxiousness, hopelessness, uncertainty, discouragement, loneliness, and even depression. We dreamed of days gone by as guidelines were redefined as to what was considered "essential" and "non-essential," while abruptly schools were closed, offices were shut down, shortages abounded, and the world hunkered down unsteadily clutching our bottles of hand sanitizer behind our locked doors, as we proudly wore our masks to prevent "the spread," all the while shaking our heads in disbelief.

Local churches were mandated to stop gathering together as congregations and were required to abandon their sanctuaries and worship online from home. Apart, we became somewhat emotionally and spiritually shaken as hospitals filled to over-capacity and we asked ourselves, "Who will be next?", while we learned terms like PPE, nasal swab testing, intubation, flattening the curve, isolation, and social distancing. Covid cases took on individual names that sadly we began to recognize, and we were broken to think of those being hospitalized—put on ventilators—losing their lives—or losing a loved one.

As some became spiritually dry, angrily shaking their fists at GOD, many began to urgently cry out to HIM in their brokenness as they remembered HIS faithfulness and mercies of the past. Fervent prayers of intercession for HIS forgiveness, deliverance, and victory were lifted as this nemesis persisted to rear its ugly head. As we continued to walk this uphill road, Covid ministry suddenly transformed into a treasured opportunity rather than a dreaded task. HIS church rose up and through her tears, found new ways to sow seeds of encouragement, comfort, and share HIS hope and salvation through JESUS CHRIST with those suffering in a dark world emotionally, physically, and spiritually drained. Prayer warriors passionately began to bind together in prayer and thanksgiving on social media, by telephone, and in Zoom meetings. Weeping with those who weep, and rejoicing at each victory for HIS glory. Amazingly, rediscovering our song in HIM while continuing to make the ascent.

For such a time as this, life as we knew it has changed, but our awesome FATHER GOD has not. Although the battle is currently not over, Isaiah 43:19 says, "Behold, I AM about to do something new; even now it is coming. Do you not see it? Indeed, I will make a way in the wilderness and streams in the desert."

Do you not see it? Indeed, HE will make a way. HE is the LIVING WATER we desperately need in this parched wilderness of Covid. GOD continues to hear our cries for deliverance, healing, and restoration. There is no one like our JEHOVAH-RAPHA, the GOD who heals. The GREAT I AM remains faithful even in this storm. The living waters of HIS salvation continue to saturate our drought stricken hearts, and our mouths are once again being filled with eternal laughter as we loudly resound our songs of joy and thanksgiving. How I love the sound of laughter and songs of joy. . .

"The LORD has done great things for them! The LORD has done great things for us"— and no doubt, HE will. To GOD be the glory!

December 20

An Advent Prayer

O God of Elizabeth and Mary,

You visited Your servants with news

of the world's redemption

in the coming of the Savior.

Make our hearts leap with joy,

and fill our mouths with songs of praise,

that we may announce glad tidings of peace,

and welcome the Christ in our midst. Amen.

God of promise,

You have given us a sign of your love

through the gift of Jesus Christ, our Savior,

Who was promised from ages past.

We believe as Joseph did

the message of Your presence

whispered by an angel,

and offer our prayers for Your world,

confident of Your care and mercy for all creation. Amen.

Shepherd of Israel,

may Jesus, Emmanuel and Son of Mary,

be more than just a dream in our hearts.

Save us, restore us,

and lead us in the way of grace and peace,

that we may bear Your promise into the world. Amen[12]

December 21

Mary's Song

Luke 1:47-55

Written by: Christy Grantham

Mary, the mother of Jesus, was a thinker. She liked to ponder things. I can relate to that. A lot of people in today's day and time ponder out loud and make a living at it as Bloggers and Influencers. I'm so glad her story was recorded for us and her inner thoughts were revealed.

Mary was chosen to carry and nurture the Son of God. That would certainly give one reason to ponder! "Me? Why me? Who am I that you would choose me? I'm afraid. I'll fail. What will people think? What will Joseph think?" She's so.... well, human. Mary worked through all of those questions and uncertainties by leaning into and depending on the Lord's grace and mercy.

Mary started this journey with belief; and not just believing what He told her, but believing in Who He is. These are two very different beliefs. It is easy to believe what someone says, but believing they will be able to follow through is another thing entirely. I believed my husband David at the altar when he said he loved me and would cherish me always, but when the marriage got tough and the living got hard, I struggled to believe he would follow through. I doubted his ability to keep his word. I'm sure he felt the same at times. It's a process and often times, in our humanness, has to be proven.

But God. That's how Mary looked at things. She knew she couldn't trust the world's opinion of her or even Joseph's word, but what she had made up her mind about was she could trust the Lord no matter what. No matter how outlandish this seemed; No matter how scandalous; No matter how incredible; No matter the rumors from her family and friends and neighbors, her trust and dependence was solely in her God. And because her trust was there in that safe place, she was able to rejoice and sing. She was able to put her worries and anxiety and questions aside and enter into perfect praise. Her faith was strengthened through the journey as a result.

Mary wasn't just God's choice to bear the Christ Child, but she was a humble follower of her Messiah. Her journey started with faith and obedience. When Gabriel came to Mary and announced that she, a virgin, would give a birth to the Messiah, she demonstrated not only obedience, but a profound understanding of the scriptures and a blind belief in her Lord. She was so caught up in her belief that she immediately rejoiced, and if she was around today her response would've been, "Let's do this thing!" (That is my interpretation of Luke 1:38.)

Like any good woman would do, Mary couldn't wait to visit with her BFF, Elizabeth, who, she learned through an angelic grapevine, was also miraculously expecting a child. Elizabeth was old and had been barren her whole life, but just like that, was expecting a blessed child! I can just hear them now squealing like little girls. I love that the Lord made women this way. (If you are a man reading this right now, indulge me for a minute.) I love that the Lord allowed them this experience together. There is just nothing on the face of this earth like loving the Lord and being able to praise Him with your best friends! It's a girl thing, and hopefully a man thing, too!

Here these two are, defying the odds together. No wonder

Mary broke out in song! If you haven't read it already, read it now. If you've read it, read it again with fresh eyes. "The Song of Mary" is also called "The Magnificat" and is found in Luke 1:47-55. At this point, Mary was just begging the Lord to be glorified through her life. She was so thankful and filled with awe that she had to sing. She recognized His mercy on her own life and on Elizabeth's.

They were living proof of prophesy fulfilled.

"As He spoke to our fathers, to

Abraham and to his seed forever."

Ponder that!

December 22

Almost There

Mark 12:28-34

"You are not far from the Kingdom of God." These are the words that Jesus spoke to a scribe who questioned Him on His last Tuesday before Calvary.

Jesus was again in the Temple in Jerusalem. It was fitting that He would be there. The Temple was the building God had established as the earthly place where He would dwell with His covenant people. And here He was, right there in their midst— the incarnate God— the One to Whom they were offering their Passover sacrifices— but they didn't recognize Him.

"You're not far…." They could have reached out and touched His garment with honor and adoration. They could have bowed in reverence at His feet. But "not far" proved to be "too far" for many of them.

The question that the scribe asked Jesus was the question of the greatest commandment. Jesus answered the question by quoting from Deuteronomy 6: "Hear, O Israel! The Lord our God is one Lord; and you shall love the Lord your God with all your heart, and with all your soul, and with all your mind, and with all your strength. The second is this: You shall love your neighbor as yourself."

"Yes," the scribe responded. "Loving God and loving our neighbors is much greater than all the burnt offerings and sacrifices." This was a good answer.

A scribe was a man who was familiar with the Law. They were the ones who interpreted Mosaic Law into practical legal matters. This man had a cognitive grasp of the truth, but what the truth meant for his own life had eluded him.

He could say that loving God was better than sacrifice, but he couldn't bring himself to say to the God Who stood before him, "I love You."

The scribe knew so much about God without ever truly knowing God Himself. And for this reason, I find there to be great sadness in the words that Jesus spoke to him. "You're not far...."

This man was right there at the threshold. He knew the power of love, the love that God desires more than every offering or sacrifice His people could ever make.

But you see, the scribe was stuck there for the same reason that many people today are stuck.

Loving God takes courage. It requires us to bow our knee to someone other than ourselves. It requires us to humble ourselves, to commit our lives in faith to the unseen God, and to put aside our own will and pray for His will to be done. And just like every other relationship, it takes doing these things every single day.

Every single day, we crown our God as King of our lives. Every single day, we proclaim Him as Lord of our lives. Every single day, we worship Him as the only One worthy of praise. Every single day, we renew our love for Him, we plead with Him to know Him more intimately, to cleanse and purify us more fully, to transform us more and more– from glory to glory.

There is much that loving God with all our heart, soul, mind, and strength requires of us that is hard to do. It is not an easy road, but it is a path of great peace and goodness. Where God's mercy and grace meets us at the point of every need. Where His faithful provisions astound us.

If we can only get there. If we can only step over that threshold from knowing about Him, to knowing Him. If we can only allow Him to rescue us from the walls of self we have built around our hearts, and from the idols of self we have placed on an altar there. If we can only move from that place of knowing that we should love Him, to loving Him.

The scribe must have been surprised by Jesus' response to him. What must he have thought when Jesus told him that he wasn't far from the Kingdom? Don't you think this man who was so well–versed in Scripture, who was among the most faithful to his religion, likely believed himself to already have been in the Kingdom? From his perspective, until Jesus uttered those words, he probably believed that he had it all figured out.

What about you today? Are you in? Or are you only close? Are you living a religious life, going through motions, knowing about Jesus without knowing Him, without truly having a relationship with Him?

Do you love Him? Truly love Him?

As we approach the manger to worship the newborn King this Christmas, let's make our hearts a place where we worship and adore our Savior, and Him alone. Linger awhile longer with Him today.

Make your heart a sanctuary of thanksgiving and
praise, loving Him with all your heart, all your soul,
all your mind, and all your strength.

December 23

More Thrilling, More Filling

Written by: John Myer

You're about to start hearing a most recognizable Christmas slogan: "Jesus is the reason for the season." We Christians coined the phrase, actually, as a way of keeping the focus off Amazon shopping carts, and multi-layered western tradition. But Christ is not only the reason for a season linked to the past, He is the reason for the present, and the reason for the developing trajectory of the future as well.

Christ is so large, the experience of both His first and second advents reach out from the scriptures to touch us even now.

- His first coming to Jerusalem was on a donkey.
  His lowliness humbles us (Zech. 9:9).
- His second coming will be on a stallion.
  His glory awes us (Rev. 19:11).

- In His first advent, words of grace proceeded from His mouth.
  They calm, comfort, and woo our wayward souls (Luke 4:22).
- In His second advent, a sword proceeds out of His mouth.
  It judges, divides, and separates our soul from our spirit (Rev. 19:15; Heb. 4:12).

- In His first appearance, His name is Jesus.

    His gentle humanity encourages us to approach and know Him (2 Cor. 10:1).
- In His second appearance, no one knows His name but Himself.

    His mysterious divinity defies easy knowledge (Rev. 19:12).

- In His first advent, He came to shed his blood for the enemies of God.

    His passion moves us unto love for Him (2 Cor. 5:14-15).
- In His second advent, He comes to shed the blood of the enemies of God.

    His vengeance moves us unto reverence (Isa. 63:1-4, 2 Cor. 5:10-11).

- In His first advent, He submitted to earthly government, and preserved its order.

    We are reminded to respect authority, for there is no authority except what comes from God (John 19:11, Rom. 13:1-4).
- In His second advent, earthly governments submit to Him, as He overthrows them.

    We are shown that all authority in heaven and earth belongs to Him (Rev. 19:15, Matt. 28:18).

The fact is, God intends for us to worship a whole Christ in all aspects, sweet and salty. Anything less yields questionable results.

I once ate a chocolate chip cookie that seemed abnormally sweet. I declined a second one. At first I wondered if the baker had added too much sugar, but then she divulged she'd actually forgotten to add salt. More than likely, she thought it wouldn't matter, because cookies ought to be sweet, anyway. But apparently, the odd antithetical ingredients of sweet and salty combine for a certain fullness of flavor. If you alter the recipe, you'll get something unbalanced.

Theology works the same way, yielding an "off"

flavor when it falls under either secular or religious

editing. The Christ God presents to us in Scripture

brings the fullness of divine and human reality

a thrilling and filling gift to all humankind.

Receive Him as He is, and truly you will find,

"You have been filled in him" (Col. 2:10).

December 24

Christmas Eve: You Better Watch Out!

Mark 13: 24-37

Tonight all over the world children (and parents) are anticipating a sleepless night. There's so much excitement waiting for Santa to come and leave those much longed for toys and gifts. Even the North American Air Defense Command (NORAD) spends Christmas Eve on a mission to "track and protect Santa and his sleigh on his trip to and from the United States against possible attack from those who don't believe in Christmas."

There are a lot of versions of how this "mission" began, but they all point to a misdialed number by a child trying to reach the North Pole, and instead reaching Col. Harry Shoup's desk phone. Today, volunteers at NORAD Santa Tracker handle 12,000 emails and 100,000 phone calls from over 200 countries on Christmas Eve from all the children who are watching for Santa.[13]

Oh that we would watch for Christ's return with as much passion as a child waiting for Santa Clause! In Mark 13, Jesus instructed us to be on the alert for His return. But His instruction wasn't that we should pass our days looking at the skies, or even analyzing the world events that He described in this passage. There is a place and a need for us to study what Scripture tells us about these things, but not from morbid curiosity. The study of what we commonly call "End Times" should compel us to a deeper sense of excitement to see Him, to throw off the earthly for the heavenly, and to enter that eternal Kingdom.

Jesus told His disciples that we each have been assigned a task to perform, we've been entrusted by the Master of the House to do the work He's left for us. Staying alert, then, means that we are to simply live in obedience to Him. His admonition to us is that we are to obey Him in light of His return— not out of fear of punishment, but out of a desire to please and honor Him. We serve God and obey Him out of the intimate relationship that we have, the relationship that He has initiated and made complete by sending His Son.

Tonight, millions of parents are going to have That Conversation with their children— "If you don't go to sleep, Santa won't come."

We never need worry that Jesus is going to skip over us if He finds us sleeping. He will come, no matter what— nothing we do can make His promises null. But watching for Him in complete obedience fills our hearts with immeasurable joy and delight. He tells us that we will "see the Son of Man coming in clouds with great power and glory. And then He will send forth the angels, and will gather together His elect from the four winds, from the farthest end of the earth to the farthest end of heaven" (verses 26-27). What an amazing sight that will be— a sight that will be etched into our memories for all of eternity.

Tonight, as you observe Christmas Eve, celebrating the night Jesus wrapped Himself in flesh and entered our world, how are you keeping alert? Are you watching for Him with great anticipation and joy? Are you daily preparing your heart to meet Him?

December 25

Christmas Morning Prayer

Lord, You have come— this is what we celebrate today. A holy God, a perfect Savior, a merciful Lord, a loving Father— choosing to become like us, choosing to live in the same flesh, the same fallen Creation as His beloved. For He will save His people from their sins— was the message the angel spoke to Joseph. It is the message of great hope for us today.

You have done it. You have saved us through Your perfect sacrifice. When we didn't even know we needed saving. When we were satisfied with the crude and shallow kindnesses of humanity because we never knew the difference between what our flesh could do and the holiness, the purity, of all that Heaven sent us when You came.

When we cried out to some unknown, some unseen, for

mercy from the things that overwhelmed us because, though we knew we needed mercy, we didn't know where it would come from. But then You came.

When we thought we knew what love was, when we pursued the happy picture of it, the only picture we knew, and still felt hollow and empty and unfulfilled and alone because we could never know what was missing— until You came.

When we pursued riches and honor and privilege and never felt satisfaction or contentment— Until You came, all the Glory of Heaven laid in a manger.

Forgive us for the frivolity that overtakes the sacred in our celebration. Forgive us for flippantly chiming that "Jesus is the Reason for the Season" and for forgetting that we are Your reason.

Oh, yes, Your great love for us. A love that saw the depth of our need for saving and chose to step out of Glory and into the dirt. To live a sinless life in the flesh to fulfill the awful and unthinkable thing that had to be done. For us.

Unto us a Child is born. Unto us a Son is given.

Let us today be the humble recipients of this greatest of gifts; let us be glad in the lavish expression of Your love for us. Let us experience the peace in our souls that became ours when You came. Let us surrender our hearts and extend our arms into Your glorious embrace.

Let us celebrate Your holiness, Your purity, Your mercy, Your love. Let us celebrate the moment You came to us. Let us fix our eyes toward the moment You will come to us again.

Observing Advent at Home

*P*arents, do your children know the story of Christmas?

Do they know that Christmas is when Jesus was born so that He could one day be the perfect sacrifice for our sins, restoring our relationship with God?

The lessons in this family section are designed to help you lead your children to a knowledge of the salvation message found in the account of Jesus' birth. It is this message that permeates the season of Advent.

We are seeing in our world an all-out war for the souls of every human being. The Word of God, through the Spirit of God, is the greatest tool that you have as a parent to make sure that your eternal destiny and that of your children is secured in Heaven.

In this book, I have shared with you how to observe the season of Advent at home with your children. I have explained the wreath and the candles below. Use these tools to help draw your focus to the true reason for Christmas and to help focus on the purpose of Advent, which is a time of preparation to meet our King.

This year, my challenge is that you give your children and family the Gospel message above all else. You can start by making sure that each member of your family owns a print Bible.

Yes, Bibles are available on phones, tablets, the Internet. And how blessed we are to live in a time where the Word of God is so readily available to us.

When we hold a Bible in our hands, though, we are holding something that is set-apart for one purpose– to deliver God's Word to our hearts. Our phones or tablets are not set-apart for that. We use them for communicating, for playing games, for social media.

Make sure that everyone has a Bible, and then make sure that everyone knows how to use it.

My second challenge to you is to take your family to church regularly. Prioritize it. Make it as certain as your attending work and your children attending school. The fellowship of believers in corporate worship can't be replaced. But it must be a priority– one that won't get bumped for a family outing or a sporting event. Go to church. It really is important.

The following lessons contain the message of Christmas. There is great power in this message. It is the power of the Gospel, and it is important for all ages to hear it. It is a message that never grows old, but grows us up in Christ every time we hear it.

The lessons are written so that you can easily adapt them for the age of the children in your family.

A good way to use the lessons is to set a specific time each week to sit down together. This can even be a weekly gathering for your small group or Sunday School class, gathering several families together for Advent lessons and activities each week.

First, say a short prayer. Then go through the lesson, making sure to ask questions about what family members remember from the week before and sharing any thoughts anyone might have had.

Then, talk about what questions your children or family members may have about the content of the message, how they can apply the message, or what thoughts or questions they may have. End with another prayer. Sample prayers are included each week. Lead your family in prayer, and then give your children the opportunity to voice their own prayers as well.

Whether you use the words I've written here, or whether you find your own, teach your children the Gospel. Teach them well, and teach them often.

The most important thing you can ever teach them is that Jesus died for them, that He rose from the dead, and that He is coming back one day. The most important thing you can show them is how to walk faithfully with God. The most important thing you can give them is the security of knowing that your family will be together in Heaven for all eternity.

May this Advent be the season your family believes.

The Advent Wreath

If you choose to incorporate an Advent Wreath into your family observance, choose a simple wreath that is covered with evergreens.

Advent wreath forms can be purchased at Hobby Lobby or online. These are outfitted with four candle holders around the circumference of the wreath form, but are only the wire frame. You will need to attach the evergreen (real or artificial).

The evergreen symbolizes God's unchanging nature. The shape of the wreath symbolizes that He is infinite.

There are four Advent candles that can be purchased as a set. Each set contains three purple candles and one pink. A fifth candle can be purchased separately. The fifth candle, usually a white pillar candle, should be placed in the center of the wreath. This is the Christ candle and is to be lit on Christmas Eve.

There are cues written within each week's lesson if you are using the Advent Wreath. Just leave those cues out if you are not using a wreath.

Weekly Family Readings

Family Week One

Why We Learn About Christmas— Where It All Began

Background passages: Genesis 1, Genesis 2:15-23, Genesis 3

This is a very special time of the year because it's the time we celebrate the birth of Jesus.

Why is Jesus' birth so important and so special?

You see, long, long ago, long before there was Christmas, God created the earth, the universe, and all the plants and animals. Everything He created was very, very good. But there was something that was still missing, and that something was people.

God created a man, Adam, and a woman, Eve. He put the man and woman in a beautiful garden and gave them everything they needed to live. The best part was that every day, Adam and Eve got to spend time with God.

God had told Adam and Eve the one rule they had to follow in the garden. There was one thing they must not ever do— that was to eat from one specific tree in the garden. God told them that if they disobeyed Him and ate from the tree, they would have to leave the garden and would one day die. If they obeyed God, their lives would be perfect. They would never be sick or hurt or sad. And they would live forever in this beautiful place with God.

God had an enemy who sneaked into the garden. That enemy was Satan. Because Satan was God's enemy, he was also an enemy of Adam and Eve. He wanted to ruin the beautiful friendship that God had with the man and woman. So Satan disguised himself as a serpent and convinced Eve that it was really okay to eat the fruit from the one tree God had told them not to eat.

When Eve, and later Adam, ate the fruit from the tree, this was called sin. They had disobeyed God, even though they knew the consequences would be very bad. It made God very sad, but because He is a very holy God, He had to keep His word. Adam and Eve had to leave the garden.

God told them all about offerings and sacrifices that they could give in order to honor and obey Him so they could still be friends, but their friendship was different now because Adam and Eve were different. More and more they wanted to choose their own way to live instead of listening and obeying God. Also, there was sickness, and sadness, and one day they would die.

You see, God wants people to love Him and obey Him. But because man chose the consequences of sin over friendship with Him, God knew that one day, He would have to come down to Earth to be the one offering and sacrifice that would finally be good enough to restore the friendship He wants to have with the people He created.

At Christmas, God sent His Son Jesus to Earth as a tiny baby. Jesus would grow up to teach people about Who God is and what God wants. He would show people how much God loves us and wants to be with us. He would give His very own life so that we can be with Him. And one day He will come back to take us to Heaven.

The Bible says that God loved the world so much that He gave His only Son, that whoever believes in Him should not perish, but have everlasting life. No one will ever love you as much as Jesus does– and that's why we learn about the true story of Christmas.

(Advent Wreath: Light a purple candle. This is an Advent Wreath that will help us think about why Jesus came to Earth, and remember that He will return. The wreath is round– it has no beginning and no end. This reminds us that God doesn't have a beginning or an end– He has always been and always will be. The wreath is covered in evergreen. This reminds us that God never changes. The candle that we are lighting tonight is meant to remind us that, because Jesus came at Christmas so that He could pay the penalty for our sins, we have hope that we can live in Heaven with Him forever. So the first candle is the hope candle.)

Let's say a prayer thanking God for creating us and for loving us. Let's ask Him to forgive us for choosing to disobey Him, and ask Him to help us always love Him and obey Him. Let's thank Him for sending Jesus so that we can have everlasting life.

Week Two

The People God Chose for His Perfect Plan

Background passage: Luke 1, Matthew 1:18-25

(Advent Wreath: Light the purple candle that was lit last week. It will stay lit as you read this lesson.)

God chose some very special people to be involved when it was time for God's Son, Jesus to come to Earth.

Before Jesus was born, God sent another baby, named John. John had an earthly mother and an earthly father– Zechariah and Elizabeth. John's parents loved God very much and obeyed God. Zechariah was a priest, which meant that he was in charge of helping people give their offerings and sacrifices to God. But they were old, past the age when anyone would expect that they would have children.

One day, an angel named Gabriel came to Zechariah and told him that his wife Elizabeth was going to have a son. At first, Zechariah didn't believe Gabriel. So the angel told Zechariah that he would not be able to speak until the child was born– this was going to be a sign that Gabriel was telling him the truth!

When John grew up he would have an important job. His job was to tell people about Jesus.

Can you think of a reason why John's job was so important? Everyone needs to know Who Jesus is– that He is the Son of God. If we don't know Jesus, then our relationship with God can never be restored. Who told you about Jesus?

There were other really important people God chose. One of those people was Mary. Mary was a young lady who was going to marry a man named Joseph. God chose Mary to be Jesus' mother. Since Jesus is God's Son, He didn't need an earthly Father. So, God made a special way for Jesus to come to earth as a baby so that His birth would be unlike any other birth.

Just a few months before John was born, the same angel, Gabriel, came to Mary and told her that she was going to have a child! Like Zechariah, Mary was amazed, since she was not yet married to Joseph. The angel explained that God would cause an amazing miracle to happen to Mary so that she could be the mother of Jesus.

An angel also told Joseph about Mary being the mother of Jesus. Hundreds of years before Jesus was born, God had told His prophets that Jesus would be born in town called Bethlehem. Joseph was a citizen of Bethlehem. When the Emperor of Rome called for everyone to be counted in their hometown, Joseph had to take Mary with him to Bethlehem so that they could be counted. See how God worked all those details out?

Every person God chose to be a part of Jesus' earthly life was special, and each one was chosen even before they were born. The plan that God made for restoring our relationship with Him is a perfect plan because Jesus Who is perfect came to be our Savior.

God has a plan for you, too. It's a plan that He chose even before you were born. He loves you with a perfect love. He loves you more than anyone else ever could, and He has every detail of His great plan for you worked out.

When you love Him and obey Him, when you spend time getting to know Him by reading your Bible and talking with Him in prayer, He will tell you just what His plan for you is.

(Advent Wreath: Light a second purple candle. Who remembers what the first purple candle reminds us of? It is the Hope candle, because when God sent His Son, He was giving us a way for us to be with Him in Heaven forever. Tonight we are lighting the second candle— it is the peace candle. We have peace when we know that God loves us and has a plan for us. We don't have to worry about anything, because no matter what happens, God has everything already worked out for us. Any time we may feel worried or afraid, we can remember that God gives us peace because He is always with us.)

Let's say a prayer, thanking God for His perfect plan. Let's thank Him that He worked out His perfect plan to send Jesus. And let's pray that we will follow the special plan that He has for our lives. Let's ask Him to help us trust Him when we feel worried or afraid, and ask Him to remind us that He is always with us.

Week Three

The Star and the Magi

Background passage: Matthew 1:1-12

(Advent Wreath: Light the two previous purple candles before you begin.)

Last week you learned about the people that God chose to be involved in Jesus' birth. Can you remember who they were? Here are some questions you can try to answer:

Who did God send as a baby who would grow up to tell other people Who Jesus is?

Who were that baby's parents?

What was that father's job?

Why did that baby's father not believe the angel who told him that he and his wife would be parents?

What happened to him when he questioned the angel?

What was the name of the young woman who would be Jesus' mother?

Why did Jesus not need an earthly father?

Who was Jesus' mother married to?

Where was Mary's husband from, and why was that important?

Where did Mary and Joseph have to go to be counted?

How can you know God's plan for your life?

Here's something very important you need to know about God: God wants everyone to know about Him!

Everyone who has ever existed— this means you, too!— was specially designed and created by God. The Bible tells us that He wants everyone to know how much He loves us. So, He sends people to tell us.

This book that you are reading is a way that He is telling you how much He loves you! This book is something that God has given you so that you can know about how He has made it possible for you to have a relationship with Him.

Now, if you ever want to know about things that are happening in the world, the main way you are going to find that out is by using the Internet, turning on the television or radio, or by calling or texting someone on your cell phone.

Of course, thousands of years ago, the Internet, televisions, radios, and telephones didn't exist. People usually found things out by hearing them from others.

When Jesus was born, though, God wanted as many people from all over the world to hear about His plan. We already know that He sent angels to Mary and Joseph, and to Zechariah and Elizabeth. But He used something else to let others around the world know about Jesus.

One night, God spoke, and a very special star appeared in the sky. In His great wisdom, He placed the star exactly where it needed to be. Then, very gently, He urged a group of stargazers in the East, the Magi (or Wise Men), to look up at the sky— right where the new star was.

The Magi saw it— just like God meant them to! It was amazing! And not only did they see the star, they studied it— and then they followed it, too. It was a long journey, and they wouldn't get to see Jesus as a newborn baby. But these Magi were going to be given a very important message to take back to the people in the area of the world where they lived.

You see, our all-knowing, all-wise God, chose the Magi to be His special messengers about the birth of Jesus. They were a very important part of letting everyone know His plan to bring us all together with Him.

Tonight, when you look at the stars, remember the God Who created each one of them also created you. Remember those Magi, and remember that God can use you, too, to tell others about His amazing love for us.

(Advent Wreath: Light the pink candle. Tonight we are lighting the pink candle. It is the Joy candle. The message of Jesus brings great joy to everyone who hears it. Even though there may be things that make us sad sometimes, we know that when we have Jesus' love in our hearts, we will always have joy. This candle also reminds us that God's heart overflows with joy because of His love for us. Just as we are looking forward to the day when Jesus will return for us, God is also looking forward to having us with Him in Heaven for all eternity.)

Let's say a prayer thanking God for making that star, so that people in another part of the world could know about Jesus. Thank Him for all the ways He makes sure you know about Him. Thank Him for your parents, your pastor, your teachers at church, who make sure that you know about Jesus. Ask Him to remind you of someone that you know who may not know how much Jesus loves them, and then ask Him to provide an opportunity for you to share that good news with them.

Week Four

What the Shepherds Heard

Luke 2:1-20

(Advent Wreath: Light the three previous candles before you begin, reminding your children what each of the candles represents.)

Now, if you had an important message to tell, say, for example, that God was coming to Earth as a newborn baby– who do you think would be the first people you would tell?

Maybe the President? Or Kings? Or Preachers? Fox News or CNN?

But guess who the angels told? Shepherds!! Amazing, isn't it? The night that Jesus was born, the angels appeared to a group of shepherds who were taking care of their flocks of sheep on the hills.

The shepherds were pretty terrified when they first saw the angel. The Bible says that the "glory of the Lord shone around" the shepherds. But the angel told them not to be afraid, because he had good news to tell them.

You probably know what the good news was!

Mary and Joseph had arrived in Bethlehem. They needed somewhere to stay. But because the town was so busy with people coming for the census, there was no room for them anywhere. This was probably very troubling to Joseph and Mary, because they knew it was time for Mary's baby to be born.

Finally, they found a stable– a place where animals (probably sheep) were kept. It was smelly and dirty, but at least there was shelter.

It was this stable where Jesus was born. There wasn't a cradle for Him, so Mary wrapped Him in cloths and laid Him in a manger. A manger is a place where the farmer would put straw and hay for the animals to eat.

When the angels told the shepherds about the birth of Jesus, they told them that Jesus' birth would bring great joy to all people, because Jesus was the Messiah, the King, that God had promised to send.

Then, there were more angels, so excited about the birth of Jesus, that they were praising God right there with the hills and sheep and shepherds!

You know, if the angels told the King, or the religious leaders first about Jesus first, then it might have been a long time for the good news of Jesus' birth to reach the shepherds. They would likely have a lot of questions, too. No one expects a King to be born in a stable, to be wrapped in cloths and placed in a manger! Kings are born in palaces!

To the shepherds, it made perfect sense, though, so the angels told them first. That always makes me really happy because it meant that God loves the lowly shepherds so much that He wanted them to be able to hear the message of Christmas right away.

Those shepherds got right up out of those fields and went and found the little baby Jesus and worshipped Him. They knew that even though He was in a dirty manger, He was exactly who the angels said He was– The Messiah, God's only Son. They knew that God had kept all His promises. And then, they were so excited that they went around to all the people in the town and told them, too.

The news of Jesus' birth is still good news today– and God has chosen you to hear about it! But none of us who hear it are meant to keep it to ourselves– we are meant to share it with others. Knowing that God sent His only Son Jesus because of His great love for us, so that He could be our Savior, brings great joy and peace to our hearts.

Do you know how much God loves you? He doesn't love you because you're pretty or handsome or smart. He doesn't love you because you're a good person. He doesn't love you because you obey your parents or get good grades in school.

God loves you because He chooses to love you– not because of who you are, but because of Who He is. This is why He sent His Son to be born on Christmas– so that one day, He could become the perfect sacrifice to make it possible for us to be with God forever.

Think about what Good News this is for you today, and then go and share it with someone else who may not know about the true story of Christmas.

(Advent Wreath: Light the final purple candle. Remind everyone what the previous candles were– hope, peace, joy. Tonight we are lighting the Love Candle. During this season of Advent we have been talking about how much God loves you– so much that He sent His Son. But remember that God wants our love, too. How much do you love Him? How do you show God that you love Him? Jesus said that if we love Him, we will obey Him. That means that we think and act and speak in ways that

please Him. How much do you love Him today?)

Let's say a prayer. What do you think we should thank God for today? Let's thank Him for telling the good news to the shepherds so that everyone could know that Jesus had been born. We should thank Him for keeping all His promises to send Jesus to be born. We should thank Him for loving us as much as He does. As we pray, think about how you show Him how much you love Him, and ask Him how you can love Him more. Thank Him for Jesus.

Christmas

(Advent Wreath: Light all four candles. Light the Christ candle in the center)

Today is Christmas– our great celebration of Jesus coming to earth.

Whether you receive many gifts or just one.

Whether you receive grand gifts or just simple.

Whether your gifts are wrapped in beautiful packages or just placed unwrapped under the tree, remember your greatest gift, that most wondrous gift, is Jesus.

When all the decorations come down, and the last bite of turkey has been eaten, Jesus will still be with you. The white candle in the center of the wreath is called the Christ Candle. Today we will leave this candle burning to remind us that He is always with us. John 1:4-5 tells us that "In Him was life, and that life was the light of all mankind. The light shines in the darkness, and the darkness has not overcome it." Today when we look at this candle, we will remember Jesus, our Savior, who came to give us eternal life.

We know that God kept His promise to send His Son Jesus, but there is another promise that we are still waiting to happen. That promise is that one day Jesus will come back, and we will see Him and everyone who loves Him and believes in Him will spend all of eternity with Him. It's a great thing to know that one day He will return to take us to Heaven with Him.

He is our Emanuel, God with us, forever and ever. He promised to never leave us, and He never will– not for all of eternity.

References

References:

[1] *Matthews, Michelle. "This Alabama Grandma Wants to Help You Fix Supper. AL.com. April 26,2020. https://www.al.com/life/2020/04/this-alabama-grandma-wants-to-help-you-fix-supper.html*

[2] *Gantt, Brenda. "Cleaning and Seasoning Iron Ware." https://www.facebook.com/cookingwithbrendagantt/videos/724056738371708*

[3] *Rose, Darlene Diebler. Evidence Not Seen. A Woman's Miraculous Faith in the Jungles of World War II. New York: Harper Collins. 1988. pp. 111, 148-150.*

[4] *Reproduced from Revised Comm on Lectionary Prayers copyright ©2002 Consultation on Common texts admin. Augsburg Fortress. Used by permission. A complete edition of the prayers is available through Augsburg Fortress.*

[5] *Zacharias, Ravi. "Hien Pham: A Man Set Apart." A Slice of Infinity. Ravi Zacharias International Ministries. 2003.*

[6] *Ridley, Jane. "I was the sole survivor of a plane crash- and spent 8 days in the jungle." NY Post. October 2, 2016. https://nypost.com/2016/10/02/i-was-the-sole-survivor-of-a-plane-crash-and-spent-7-days-in-the-jungle/*

[7] *Preaching the Word. 2 Corinthians. Power in Weakness. R. Kent Hughes, (Crossway: Wheaton, 2006), p.100*

[8] *Reproduced from Revised Common Lectionary Prayers copyright ©2002 Consultation on Common texts admin. Augsburg Fortress. Used by permission. A complete edition of the prayers is available through Augsburg Fortress.*

[9] *Roseveare, Helen. (2017) Count it All Joy. Ross-shire, Scotland: Christian Focus Publications.*

[10] *Kornei, Katherine. "Spark of Life." Discover Magazine. Dec. 19, 2016. https://www. discovermagazine.com/health/spark-of-life*

[11] *Hamilton, Robert C., M.D. 7 Secrets of the Newborn. New York: St. Martin's Press. 2018. Pages 38-39.*

[12] *Reproduced from Revised Common Lectionary Prayers copyright ©2002 Consultation on Common texts admin. Augsburg Fortress. Used by permission. A complete edition of the prayers is available through Augsburg Fortress.*

[13] *"NORAD Tracks Santa." Wikipedia, The Free Encyclopedia. 14 July 2020. https:// en.wikipedia.org/wiki/NORAD_Tracks_Santa.*

About the Author

Dr. Chrissie Tomlinson is the author of the inspirational blog This Road Home. She resides in Perry, Georgia.

Contact information:

 thisroadhomeblog@gmail.com

 thisroadhome.com